People in My Community

Doctors

By Jacqueline Laks Gorman

Gareth Stevens
Publishing

Please visit our Web site, www.garethstevens.com. For a free color catalog of all our high-quality books, call toll free 1-800-542-2595 or fax 1-877-542-2596.

Library of Congress Cataloging-in-Publication Data

Gorman, Jacqueline Laks, 1955-
 Doctors / Jacqueline Laks Gorman.
   p. cm. – (People in my community)
 Includes index.
 ISBN 978-1-4339-3804-7 (pbk.)
 ISBN 978-1-4339-3805-4 (6-pack)
 ISBN 978-1-4339-3803-0 (library binding)
 1. Physicians—Juvenile literature. 2. Medicine—Juvenile literature. I. Title.
 R690.G662 2011
 610.92—dc22
                           2010013211

New edition published 2011 by
Gareth Stevens Publishing
111 East 14th Street, Suite 349
New York, NY 10003

New text and images this edition copyright © 2011 Gareth Stevens Publishing

Original edition published 2003 by Weekly Reader® Books
An imprint of Gareth Stevens Publishing
Original edition text and images copyright © 2003 Gareth Stevens Publishing

Art direction: Haley Harasymiw, Tammy Gruenwald
Page layout: Daniel Hosek, Katherine A. Goedheer
Editorial direction: Kerri O'Donnell, Diane Laska Swanke

Photo credits: Cover, p. 1, back cover Thomas Northcut/Digital Vision/Getty Images; pp. 5, 9, 17, 19, 21 Shutterstock.com; p. 13 Joe Raedle/Getty Images; pp. 7, 15 Gregg Andersen; p. 11 Tim Boyle/ Getty Images.

Printed in the United States of America

CPSIA Compliance Information: Batch #CR011011GS: For further information contact Gareth Stevens, New York, New York at 1-800-542-2595.

Table of Contents

What Is a Doctor? 4

A Doctor's Tools. 6

Where Doctors Work 16

Glossary. 22

For More Information. 23

Index 24

Boldface words appear in the glossary.

What Is a Doctor?

A doctor is someone who helps you stay healthy. A doctor also helps you when you are sick.

A Doctor's Tools

When you visit the doctor, he checks your **temperature**. He uses a **thermometer**.

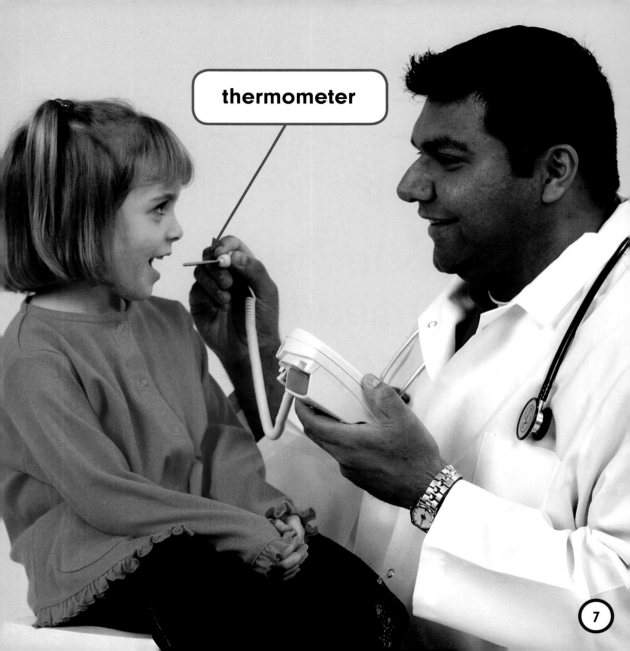

The doctor listens to your heart with a **stethoscope**. He listens to your breathing, too.

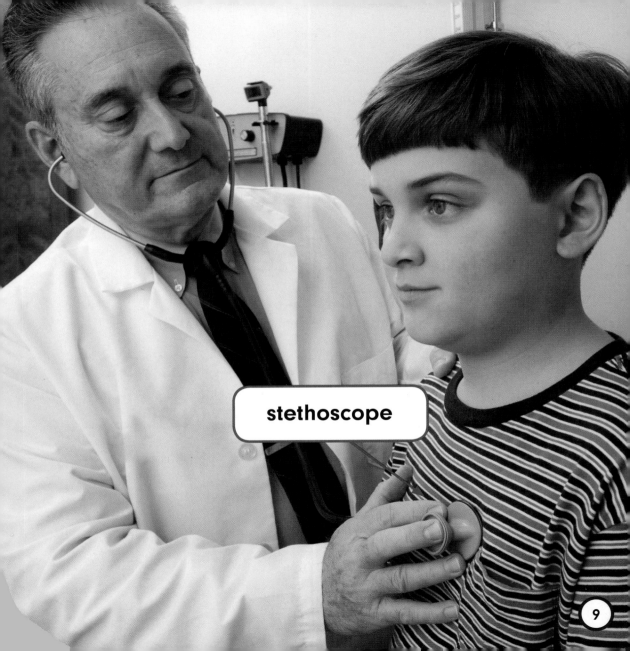

stethoscope

The doctor checks to see how much you weigh. She wants to see how you are growing.

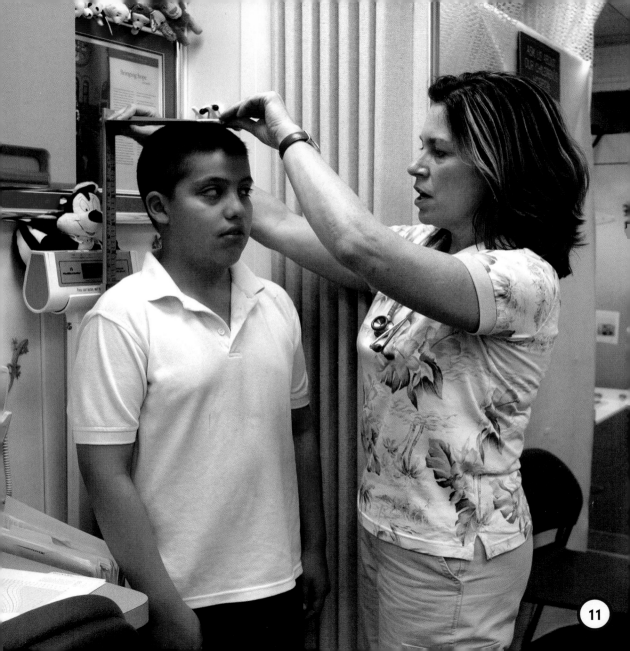

The doctor also checks inside your ears, nose, and throat. The doctor uses an **otoscope**.

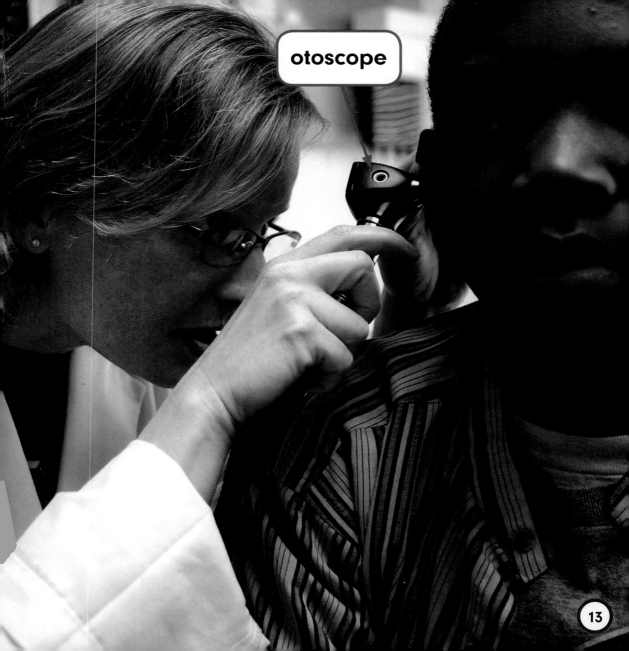

otoscope

13

Sometimes the doctor gives you a shot. This might hurt a little, but it can help you stay healthy.

Where Doctors Work

Some doctors work in hospitals. Some doctors work in offices or **clinics**.

You should visit your doctor once a year. You will get a **checkup** to be sure that you stay healthy.

Doctors help people. Do you think you would like to be a doctor someday?

Glossary

checkup: a check by a doctor to see if someone is healthy

clinic: a place where doctors see people who are sick

otoscope: a tool with a light that is used to see inside the ear, nose, and throat

stethoscope: a tool used to hear the heart and listen to breathing

temperature: how hot or cold something is

thermometer: a tool used to measure hot and cold

For More Information

Books

Buckley, James. *A Day with a Doctor*. Mankato, MN: Child's World, 2008.

Mattern, Joanne. *I Use Math at the Doctor's*. Milwaukee, WI: Weekly Reader Early Learning Library, 2006.

Web Sites

Going to the Doctor

kidshealth.org/kid/feel_better/people/going_to_dr.html
This site gives information about visiting the doctor's office. It also tells about what tools a doctor uses and their purpose.

KidsHealth

kidshealth.org/kid
This site provides facts and activities about how the body works.

Publisher's note to educators and parents: Our editors have carefully reviewed these Web sites to ensure that they are suitable for students. Many Web sites change frequently, however, and we cannot guarantee that a site's future contents will continue to meet our high standards of quality and educational value. Be advised that students should be closely supervised whenever they access the Internet.

Index

breathing 8

checkup 18

clinics 16

ears 12

healthy 4, 14, 18

heart 8

hospitals 16

nose 12

offices 16

otoscope 12, 13

shot 14

sick 4

stethoscope 8, 9

temperature 6

thermometer 6, 7

throat 12

weigh 10

About the Author

Jacqueline Laks Gorman is a writer and editor. She grew up in New York City and began her career working on encyclopedias and other reference books. Since then, she has worked on many different kinds of books. She lives with her husband and children, Colin and Caitlin, in DeKalb, Illinois.